Doudna, Kelly,

SandCastle 2

Sentences

Adjectives

Kelly Doudna

ABDO
Publishing Company

Published by SandCastle™, an imprint of ABDO Publishing Company, 4940 Viking Drive, Edina, Minnesota 55435.

Printed in the United States.

Photo credits: Comstock, Digital Stock, Eyewire Images, Image 100, Rubber Ball

Library of Congress Cataloging-in-Publication Data

Doudna, Kelly, 1963-
    Adjectives / Kelly Doudna.
       p. cm. -- (Sentences)
    Includes index.
    ISBN 1-57765-617-2
      1. English language--Adjective--Juvenile literature. [1. English language--Adjective.]
I. Title.

PE1241 .D68 2001
428.2--dc21

                                                2001022887

The SandCastle concept, content, and reading method have been reviewed and approved by a national advisory board including literacy specialists, librarians, elementary school teachers, early childhood education professionals, and parents.

Let Us Know

After reading the book, SandCastle would like you to tell us your stories about reading. What is your favorite page? Was there something hard that you needed help with? Share the ups and downs of learning to read. We want to hear from you! To get posted on the Abdo Publishing Company Web site, send us email at:

sandcastle@abdopub.com

About SandCastle™

Nonfiction books for the beginning reader

- Basic concepts of phonics are incorporated with integrated language methods of reading instruction. Most words are short, and phrases, letter sounds, and word sounds are repeated.

- Readability is determined by the number of words in each sentence, the number of characters in each word, and word lists based on curriculum frameworks.

- Full-color photography reinforces word meanings and concepts.

- "Words I Can Read" list at the end of each book teaches basic elements of grammar, helps the reader recognize the words in the text, and builds vocabulary.

- Reading levels are indicated by the number of flags on the castle.

  Note: Some pages in this book contain more than ten words in order to more clearly convey the concept of the book.

Look for more SandCastle books in these three reading levels:

Level 1 (one flag)	**Level 2** (two flags)	**Level 3** (three flags)
Grades Pre-K to K 5 or fewer words per page	**Grades K to 1** 5 to 10 words per page	**Grades 1 to 2** 10 to 15 words per page

Adjectives

An adjective is a word that describes something.

Adjectives

I play on the black swing.

It is an old tire.

Adjectives

I have a little dog.

He is white.

Adjectives

I wear a striped shirt.

I throw a yellow ball.

Adjectives

I walk next to my older brother.

He is tall.

Adjectives

My sister and I have dark hair.

Adjectives

I have fun climbing on the big rock.

Adjectives

Snow is cold.

My blue snowsuit is warm.

Adjectives

How would you describe some things in this picture?

(big, green, yellow)

Words I Can Read

Nouns

A noun is a person, place, or thing

adjective (AJ-ik-tiv) p. 5
ball (BAWL) p. 11
brother (BRUHTH-ur) p. 13
dog (DAWG) p. 9
fun (FUHN) p. 17
hair (HAIR) p. 15
picture (PIK-chur) p. 21
rock (ROK) p. 17

shirt (SHURT) p. 11
sister (SISS-tur) p. 15
snow (SNOH) p. 19
snowsuit
  (SNOH-soot) p. 19
swing (SWING) p. 7
tire (TIRE) p. 7
word (WURD) p. 5

Plural Nouns

A plural noun is more than one
person, place, or thing

things (THINGZ) p. 21

Verbs

A verb is an action or being word

climbing (KLIME-ing) p. 17

describe (di-SKRIBE) p. 21

describes
  (di-SKRIBEZ) p. 5

have (HAV) pp. 9, 15, 17

is (IZ) pp. 5, 7, 9, 13, 19

play (PLAY) p. 7

throw (THROH) p. 11

walk (WAWK) p. 13

wear (WAIR) p. 11

would (WUD) p. 21

Adjectives

An adjective describes something

big (BIG) pp. 17, 21

black (BLAK) p. 7

blue (BLOO) p. 19

cold (KOHLD) p. 19

dark (DARK) p. 15

green (GREEN) p. 21

little (LIT-uhl) p. 9

my (MYE) pp. 13, 15, 19

old (OHLD) p. 7

older (OHLD-ur) p. 13

some (SUHM) p. 21

striped (STRYPT) p. 11

tall (TAWL) p. 13

this (THISS) p. 21

warm (WORM) p. 19

white (WITE) p. 9

yellow (YEL-oh) pp. 11, 21

Match each picture to the adjective that describes something about it

big
cold
striped
yellow